FIFTY WAYS TO PRACTICE READING

Tips for ESL/EFL Students

BELINDA YOUNG-DAVY

CONTENTS

HOW TO USE THIS BOOK

It takes many hours to become proficient at anything – a sport, a hobby, a musical instrument, or a foreign language. Many thousands of hours, in fact! For a student of English, this can seem difficult to accomplish, especially if your only opportunity to study English is in the classroom.

This book will help you practice reading in English, both inside and outside the classroom. If you are already taking English classes, some of the tips will help you get more out of your classes. If you're not taking English classes – and even if you are – other tips will give you ideas to try on your own. Not every idea will work for every student. That's why there are fifty. We feel sure that many of the ideas presented here will bring you results if you try them sincerely.

Here is a suggested method for using this book:

1. Read through all of the fifty ways without stopping.
2. Read through the tips again. Choose five or six that

you think might work for you. Decide when you
will try them, and for how long.

3. Try to choose different types of ideas: some that
you can use in the classroom, some that you can use
on your own. You can choose some ideas that
require going online or using media, and some that
don't. Also, choose some that you can practice with
a friend or language learning partner, and some that
you can do alone.

4. Each time you use one of the ways, make a note
about how well it worked for you and why.
Remember that most of the tips will work best if
you practice them several times (or even make
them a habit). Don't try a tip only once and decide
it's no good for you. Give the tips you try a few
chances, at least.

5. Every few weeks, read through the ways again, and
choose some new ones.

Discontinue using any methods that are not working
for you.

The most important advice, though, is to actually *do* the
suggestions you read about here. Wishing is not working. If
you don't do the work, you won't see the results.

Finally, consider trying some of the other books in our *50
Ways to Practice* series. No one skill in English is really separate from the others. Speaking, listening, reading, writing,
vocabulary, and grammar are all connected. Improving in
one area will almost always bring improvements to other
areas too.

Note: We have priced these *50 Ways to Practice* very cheaply, because we want education and learning to be available to as many people as possible. However, our authors are highly qualified professionals who work hard to create these books. If these books are useful to you, please recommend them to your friends – but please do not share them freely. Our authors will continue to write excellent and cheap books for you if they make a little money. That way, we all win. Thank you for your support! If you have comments or suggestions (such as ideas for future books that you would find useful), feel free to contact the publisher at editor@wayzgoosepress.net or join us on Facebook.

❧ I ❧
GOOD HABITS

❧ I ❧
ALWAYS HAVE SOMETHING
TO READ

There are probably many times during the day when you could read something—if you had something to read! Make it a habit to always have something with you.

Carry a magazine, ereader, or phone with English books or articles with you whenever you can. You can do a little reading on the bus or while waiting for appointments.

❧ 2 ❧

CHOOSE WELL

It's frustrating to try to read something that is too hard. It's okay to pick something that's a little bit above your level, but if you are checking every third word in a dictionary, it will be hard to follow the text.

A good method to choose a book or article that will be easy to read is by looking at two paragraphs anywhere in the article/book. Read the paragraphs and count how many words you do not know or cannot guess. If the number is less than six, it is a good article/book to read for fun and fluency.

Of course, if you have to absolutely read something for your job or because you need the information, you can just copy it into a document and use an online translator. But that is "getting information," not "getting better at reading in English." Choose realistic texts when you are working on your skills.

✻ 3 ✻
START EASY

Start by reading material that is easy for you—perhaps short magazine articles, graded readers, or even children's books.

If you don't have to stop and look up any words in a dictionary, and all of the grammar is familiar to you, you will gradually increase your reading speed. Sometimes you want to 'work' a bit when you read, but not every time! Just relaxing and reading without effort is important too.

❦ 4 ❦

SET NEW GOALS EACH MONTH

For a little more of a challenge, every month try to read one article/book that is a little bit above your reading level.

Choose a longer article or, using the method in tip #2, choose an article or book that has seven to ten words you do not know or cannot guess. This will help you improve faster than *only* reading articles/books that are easy for you.

Choose a few vocabulary words that you had to look up, and commit to learning those words. Because the reading will be a little more difficult, choose an article or story about something you are really interested in or already have some information about.

5

READ EVERYWHERE

Keep an English magazine or two in rooms where you sit (living room, kitchen, bedroom?). Read a little bit when you come into those rooms.

When you eat breakfast or take a coffee/tea break, have a newspaper or magazine nearby and read a few short articles. You can also check some online news sites on your phone.

Keep a few different types of English books and other materials by your bed at night, so you can read whatever you are in the mood for. Even a few pages every night will help!

❧ 6 ❧

READ ANYTHING

If you live in a country where English is not spoken, look for English everywhere; for example, in advertisements, on product packages, on TV advertisements, and on posters and billboards.

Make it a game by giving yourself one point for each place you see English. Every day, try to beat your previous score! You can also compete with friends.

❧ 7 ☙

CHANGE YOUR SETTINGS

Set your email program and other websites you regularly use to English. That way you will get a little English reading practice every time you log on.

Most cell phones let you change the operating language. Change yours to English! Now the basic directions for almost every app you use will appear in English. Since you probably already know how to use your apps, the language won't be too hard, but you might learn some new vocabulary or phrases. And since you will be seeing them frequently, it will be easy to remember them.

❧ II ❧
FINDING MATERIAL

❧ 8 ❧

READ ADVICE COLUMNS

Many newspapers and news sites have advice columns. Some popular ones include *Dear Abby, Dear Prudence, Miss Manners*, and *Ask Caroline*.

Read the problem and predict what advice will be given. Imagine what vocabulary will be used. Then evaluate the advice—did you agree or disagree with it?

Here are some links to advice columns:

https://slate.com/tag/advice
Check here for columns by Miss Manners. The page also categorizes past advice columns by topic, so you can choose what kind of issue to read about.

https://www.makeuseof.com/free-online-advice-columns-get-help-experts
This is a collection of different types of advice sites, with a description of each one.

✤ 9 ✤

READ INSTRUCTIONS

Read English instructions, manuals, and how-to books for things that you already know how to do—such as recipes, a driver's manual, or computer software instructions. You won't worry about comprehension as much, so you can focus on fluency and new vocabulary.

After you read several instructions, you will probably notice some repeated vocabulary and grammar. For example, instructions are often in the imperative (*Do this! Be careful not to do that!*).

For extended practice in reading, writing, and the academic subject area of choice, why not take a MOOC? A Massive Open Online Course! These university-level courses are taught online by university professors, and they are usually completely free! You do not need to be fluent in English to take a MOOC, but you will need at least an intermediate level. Because classes are free, it's also okay to start one and not finish it, if you find it too difficult or just not interesting to you.

This site lists currently available MOOCs:

https://www.mooc-list.com/

Information about MOOCs, including a description of what they are, how they work, and how to take them successfully can be found in our book *How to Be a Successful MOOC Student*, available in both ebook and paperback. For more information, check here:

https://wayzgoosepress.com/authors/-maggie-sokolik/#mooc

🦁 10 ♋

READ YOUR HOROSCOPE

Horoscopes are short and often repeat sentence structures and vocabulary, so they are a good source of short practice.

Go online and find an astrology website in English (if you have access to a print newspaper in English, you can also read horoscopes there).

Read your horoscope every day. Read your friends' horoscopes, too. Notice what verb tenses are used the most (present tense and future tenses) and what types of events they describe.

❧ 11 ❧
READ NEWS REPORTS

Set your Internet homepage to a magazine or news website that changes daily (or more often), so you read new content every time you open your browser.

If you read a short news article that is interesting, try to find a longer article about that news story at another online news site.

If reading the news is challenging, read it first in your native language. If you read news stories about the same topics, you will learn important vocabulary quickly and review it often.

❧ 12 ❧

LOOK FOR FREE BOOKS

You can easily find and download free English short stories and books from online retailers. Some books are permanently free, and some go on sale for a short period of time.

Older books that are in the *public domain* should be permanently free. Here is a good place to find public domain books. However, since these are classics, they are sometimes more difficult for language learners to read.

https://www.gutenberg.org/

Contemporary books are sometimes on sale or free for a limited time; this means that the selection is constantly changing. If you can't find a good book one day, try again another day. If a book is not interesting, don't be afraid to delete it and look for another one.

There are also email services that email you lists of free and discounted ebooks every day. Some of these include

- http://freebooksy.com
- http://robinreads.com
- http://ereadernewstoday.com
- https://www.thefussylibrarian.com/

These services are free to subscribe to.

For paperback books, don't forget your local library! Many libraries also lend ebooks.

SUBSCRIBE TO AN ELECTRONIC SOURCE

Subscribe to an electronic newsletter for an organization or person (such as an author) that you are interested in. Regular reading material will appear free in your email inbox!

When you get tired of one source, unsubscribe and try a new one.

Here are two especially good ones that feature interesting articles:

https://nowiknow.com/

https://www.understandably.com/

❧ 14 ❧
READ BLOGS

Find and subscribe to a blog about a topic you are interested in. When you subscribe to a blog, you will get a notification when there are new posts. By reading on the same subject regularly, you will increase your vocabulary in that field.

Some blogs allow comments as well, so you can interact with other regular readers.

You can easily find blogs by searching online for "blog + (that topic)."

Perhaps someday you will feel like creating your own blog in English!

15

READ EMAILED ADVERTISEMENTS

Yes, advertising can be annoying... but it can also be useful to a language learner!

Practice scanning by subscribing to an Internet retailer's newsletter. They will send you advertisements regularly. Some sites ask you to you choose how often to receive ads, such every day? once a week? only when they have a sale?

Ask yourself questions such as *What is the most expensive item they're advertising? What is the cheapest? If I could buy only one thing, what would I choose?*

Notice which words and structures occur the most often.

❧ III ❧
READING STRATEGIES

❧ 16 ❧

PRACTICE PRE-READING

Pre-reading is an important reading comprehension skill for non-fiction, especially for advanced readers or to read assignments for school. It will prepare you to better understand the information you are going to read.

Before you read the whole text, read the title, all of the headings (small section titles inside the article), and the introduction and conclusion paragraphs.

This will give you a good idea of the author's main ideas before you read the whole article.

Of course, this is a strategy for non-fiction only, not for fiction.

USE SKIMMING

Practice skimming (reading quickly for main ideas and overall impressions). Use a paper newspaper or magazine, or an online news site.

Choose one article and answer these questions:

- *What is the author's name* (if there is one)?
- *How long is the article* (be careful! It might continue on other pages)?
- *What is it mainly about?*
- *Is it mainly factual, mainly opinion, or both?*

Skimming is useful for reading long non-fiction texts. By practicing skimming on shorter texts, you will get faster and better at it.

❧ 18 ❧

USE SCANNING

Teach yourself to scan (read quickly for specific information) faster by choosing a piece of information you want to know, and finding it as quickly as you can on the Internet (or other printed resource).

For example, ask yourself, *What is the capital of Bhutan?* or *How many people lived in Tokyo in 1966?* or *What's the average lifespan of a horse?*

Time how long it takes you to find the answer. If you have a friend, you can have a race!

Scanning is a useful strategy for finding specific information, and it's also useful on tests that feature longer reading passages, such as the TOEFL. When you read a question about a detail, you can quickly find it in a long text.

Like with skimming, the more you practice scanning, the faster and better at it you will be.

❧ 19 ❧

USE WHAT YOU ALREADY KNOW

Read articles or books on topics you're familiar with. Because the ideas and information will already be familiar, this will help with speed and fluency. You might already know the important vocabulary in English, but if you don't, look it up in a dictionary and learn it.

Read about the same subject in different books or magazines or from different online sites. Compare and contrast the information and opinions.

❧ 20 ❧

ANTICIPATE AND PREDICT

Anticipating and predicting are closely tied to both reading comprehension and improving reading speed.

When you're reading non-fiction, read the first sentence and last sentence of a paragraph before you read the whole paragraph. Try to predict what the author will say or what you think will happen in the paragraph.

If you are reading a book, predict what the author will focus on in the next chapter. The chapter title will help you with this.

It doesn't matter if you guess correctly or not—just the act of predicting helps you focus on what you are reading, and will help you remember the answer.

You can use this technique with fiction, too. At the end of a chapter, predict what will happen in the next chapter. What will happen to different characters? Can you guess how the whole story will end?

❧ 21 ❧

USE A KEY WORDS STRATEGY

Look for "key words" in the article/story—the most important words in the reading, the ones that you need to know in order to understand the text.

Key words are often found in the title, topic sentences, and sentences that explain the author's main idea or thesis.

Of course, if there are any words that you think are key words but you don't know the meaning of, check them in a dictionary before you read.

❧ 22 ❧

READ MORE THAN ONE
BOOK/ARTICLE ON THE SAME
TOPIC

Books on the same topic will have a lot of the same vocabulary. That means the second and third ones you read will be easier than the first.

In addition, try to read different types of texts about the same subject; for example, a magazine article and a book, a short story and a poem, or a serious article and a funny article. You will learn and reinforce important vocabulary for the subject, and also practice identifying tone.

❧ 23 ☙

READ DIFFERENT TYPES OF TEXTS

Different kinds of texts are sometimes referred to as different *genres*. Each genre has different features.

Try reading different genres such as:

- novels
- short stories
- articles
- letters
- blogs
- advertisements
- Wikipedia entries
- social media posts
- Internet forums
- poems
- magazines
- newspapers

Notice differences in styles and tone and organization.

Different types of texts also call for different reading strategies. For example, if you are reading a long article or story for an assignment, it is not a good idea to read every word, such as every adjective or adverb. However, if you are reading for pleasure or to improve your vocabulary, take more time to read adjectives and adverbs.

❧ 24 ❧

READ ALOUD

Choose a short passage (a few paragraphs or less) and read it aloud.

Reading aloud makes you focus on each word. Practice the same passage several times, until you can read it easily and with expression. Pay attention to punctuation, too, and remember to pause for a short time after every comma and for a longer time after every period.

If you feel foolish reading aloud to yourself, try reading to someone—or something!—else. Read to your friend, a child, or even a plant or a stuffed animal. It might be a little silly, but if it helps your English, who cares?

INCREASE YOUR READING SPEED

Work to increase your reading speed. When you can read more quickly, it will probably also feel like a more pleasant experience.

Pick a paragraph in English and time yourself when you read it. Work up to reading a paragraph of about the same length in half the time.

Set a goal and try this with a friend to see who reaches the goal first. (Be sure, though, that you are not reading so fast that you lose comprehension!)

❧ 26 ❧

USE A TIMER

Commit to reading for a short period of time every day—for example, ten minutes when you wake up, or 15 minutes before you go to bed at night. Set a timer for the amount of time you chose, and read until it goes off.

Short, regular practice will bring you real results.

❧ 27 ❧

READ CAPTIONS AND SUBTITLES

One way to work on reading speed is to watch a TV show, movie, or short video in English that has captions.

Most streaming services have captions available. On YouTube, look for the CC symbol at the bottom of a video —this stands for closed captioning.

As you listen to the video, read the captions. Hearing the words will help you focus. Because the captions will appear at almost the same speed that people are talking, they can go by very fast! This will help you increase your reading speed.

If you want something a little slower, find a song on YouTube that has the lyrics on screen.

❧ 28 ❧

USE BACKGROUND INFORMATION

When reading about an unfamiliar topic, get some background information first.

Look for information in your own language about the topic before you read about it in English.

If there are words in your language that you don't know in English, check them in a dictionary before you begin reading. That will help you to read faster and with better comprehension.

❧ 29 ❧

SUMMARIZE WHAT YOU READ

Read a news story or short magazine article and then summarize it in your head, like this: *The article was about ___* (topic). *The main idea was ___* (thesis). *The writer wanted people to ___* (purpose). *The article was written for ___* (audience).

If you cannot summarize easily, that is a sign that you maybe didn't really understand what you read. Go back and read it again, and check a few words you didn't know in the dictionary. Then try summarizing again.

If you are studying for a test, write your summary on paper. Then you will have good notes to study from!

✣ 30 ✣

USE YOUR NATIVE LANGUAGE

Read a story in English that you've already read in your native language. You won't worry about comprehension, so you can focus on fluency, new vocabulary and idioms, and sentence structure.

You might notice that reading a familiar story in English feels different. Every language has a "personality." No one language is better than another, but if you can read in two languages, you will have two different experiences with the same book.

One university student of mine the first Harry Potter novel in English after she had already read it in her native Japanese. She was surprised to find that the names of the magic spells had a meaning—this was easier for her to see when she saw the words in English. The spell names are made up by the author, but she gave them roots that sound close to Latin, which many English words are based on.

❧ 31 ❧

READ IN TWO LANGUAGES

Find a short story in English that is also available in your native language (search for "bilingual stories Spanish English," for example). Read both at the same time. You can do this chapter by chapter, or even page by page or paragraph by paragraph.

You won't worry about comprehension, so you can focus grammar and style. Notice how ideas in your language are expressed in English.

32

READ IT AGAIN

Here are some reasons to read something a second (or aaa third, or a fourth!) time.

Because comprehension is easier, you can focus on fluency and speed, and also more subtle ideas such as tone.

You may also notice useful vocabulary that you did not notice the first time.

Re-reading will also help you better remember information that you may be tested on later.

You can re-read something like a textbook passage the same day (for example, once in class and then again when you get home) or later in the same week. You can also re-read a book several months later. Try to finish reading it in less time. Can you read it now without using a dictionary?

❧ 33 ❧

USE HIGHLIGHTING

When reading an article, underline or highlight one or two important ideas in every paragraph.

Notice where in the paragraph important information tends to occur. Also notice different techniques that writers use to support and expand on their topic sentences.

If you are reading an article online, print a copy so that you can highlight it. You might want to first select the article and copy it into a document, so that when you print, you don't also print a lot of advertising, which uses a lot of paper (advertisements are also usually in color—and color ink is more expensive).

❦ 34 ❦

TALK ABOUT IT

Teachers often ask students to discuss what they read with a partner or group, but you can use this strategy even outside the classroom.

Find a friend or another student, and agree to read the same thing and then discuss it.

Knowing that you will have to give your opinion about something, and explain and support that opinion, means that you will read more carefully. You might also need to look up some vocabulary to use in a discussion that was a not actually used in the reading.

❧ IV ❧

HANDLING VOCABULARY

❧ 35 ❧

USE CONTEXT

To figure out vocabulary from context (important if you don't have a dictionary, or if you don't have time to look up every word you don't know), look for context clues—words in the same sentence and the sentences before and after that give hints about what the word could mean.

Look at the part of speech—is it an adjective, adverb, noun, or verb? Suffixes (parts of a word that come at the end) sometimes show you this—words that end in *-tion*, for example, are usually nouns, and words that end in *-ive* are often adjectives.

See if there are any word roots that remind you of words you already know. If you know that *fiction* is something that is not true, and that *-ous* means something is an adjective, can you guess what *fictitious* means?

Pay attention to connectors that show contrast (such as *unlike*) because the word you don't know might be the opposite of another word in the sentence.

Check punctuation. Sometimes word definitions are given in parentheses, between dashes, or between commas after the word *or*:

- The jaguarundi (a type of wild cat) lives in Central and South America.
- Bats use echolocation—a system of making sounds and listening to the sound waves bounce back off an object—to find their way in the dark.
- The filbert, or hazelnut, is grown in both Europe and North America,

This is an important skill to develop. Native speakers do not look up every word they do not understand, and neither should you.

❧ 36 ❧

INCREASE YOUR VOCABULARY

Occasionally, read articles on topics you're not familiar with. This will help you encounter new vocabulary. (This is especially useful if you are preparing for tests such as the TOEFL iBT.)

If you find useful new words, write them down in a notebook. See if you run into the same words again as you continue to work on your reading.

It is possible to find long vocabulary lists online (for example, the Academic Word List), but it is more useful to find words in something you read because then you also see the context and how it is used.

❧ 37 ❧

READ WITHOUT A DICTIONARY

Challenge yourself to a "no dictionary" book! Choose a book at about your level or one that is a little easy, and read it without using the dictionary at all. Put your phone in another room so you are not tempted!

Reading this way will help you get used to figuring out words from context. You will also learn which words are not really important and are okay to just skip over.

❧ 38 ❧

LIMIT DICTIONARY USE

To train yourself to identify which words are the most important to learn, choose a time when you will limit your dictionary use.

For example, in half an hour, allow yourself to look up only five words. Even if there are twelve words you don't know, choose only five that you will look up later.

Write down the words, and then look them up and copy their definitions. Then, note whether the words were useful for overall comprehension or not.

If you practice this strategy, you will get better at choosing the most important words to look up. Remember that nouns and verbs are usually the most useful vocabulary for overall comprehension, followed by adjectives and adverbs.

🎋 39 🎋

LOOK IT UP TWICE

Look up a word that you think will be the most useful for you two times:

1. First, look it up in a bilingual dictionary for the meaning.
2. Next, look it up in an English-English dictionary to see how the word is used, and what words are often used with it.

You might want to check more than one English-only dictionary, since each one will be just a little different. Make sure you find one that uses the word in an example sentence. Some online dictionaries also provide a recorded pronunciation of the word, which can be useful.

❧ 40 ❧

FOCUS ON USEFUL VOCABULARY

Look up words in your dictionary that you have seen several times in a week. They are probably important or common words.

If you use vocabulary cards to study vocabulary, these are good words to choose. Write more than one example sentence using the new word on your vocabulary card—for example, copy one sentence from the dictionary, and then write one original sentence.

It's okay to not learn every word in English! An average 20-year old native speaker of English knows about 42,000 words—but only uses about 20,000 of them regularly. But full dictionaries contain over 150,000 words. If you meet an uncommon word that does not seem useful to you, save your time and energy, and let that word go. Concentrate on more common, useful words.

❧ V ❧
WORKING WITH LONGER TEXTS

WHO? WHAT? WHERE? WHEN?
WHY? HOW?

Before you start reading, write 3-4 questions you want to be able to answer after you finish reading an article or story.

Here are some good questions to start with for fiction:

- *Who are the most important people in the story?*
- *Why are they important?*
- *When did the story happen?*
- *Why is the time/location of the story important?*
- *What is the author's message?*

Here are some questions for non-fiction:

- *Who is the audience?*
- *What is the author's point of view or message?*
- *Why did the author write this (what is its purpose)?*
- *How do I know (or how can I find out) that what the author wrote is true/accurate?*

These questions will help focus your reading.

﹩ 42 ﹩

ANNOTATE LONGER ARTICLES

Have you ever been reading a long article, and then realized after a few pages that you can't remember anything about what you just read? Here is a good way to prevent that!

Write a short summary (just a sentence or two) of each paragraph. This can work better than highlighting because it makes you put the ideas into your own words—and you can't do that unless you really understand them.

If possible, write your annotations next to the paragraph on the page. If you can't, then write on a separate sheet of paper.

If you need the information in the article to study for a test or prepare for a class discussion, your annotated notes will be a big help.

❧ 43 ❧

READ ENGLISH STUDY GUIDES

There are different series of inexpensive guides in English to help students understand difficult or classic pieces of literature. Two of the most well-known are CliffsNotes and SparkNotes. They summarize the plot chapter by chapter, and also explain each character and major themes of the book. They also feature discussion and study questions for practice.

There are a few ways you can take advantage of these guides:

1. If you want to read a famous work of English literature but think it will be too hard, you can read the CliffsNotes/SparkNotes version of the book instead.

2. Read the CliffsNotes/SparkNotes version first and then read the longer book. This way you will already understand the plot or main ideas of the

book, so you can focus on vocabulary, grammar and improving your reading speed.

3. Read the CliffsNotes/SparkNotes versions and the longer book at the same time. You can check your comprehension chapter by chapter.

(Note that these guides are not available free, although your local library might have them. However, they are usually not very expensive.)

❧ 44 ❧
KEEP A READING RESPONSE JOURNAL

If you are reading a long text, and especially if you are reading several articles on the same subject, keep a response journal. You can do this on paper or type a document.

After every few paragraphs, stop and briefly summarize the most important ideas (this will be even easier if you have been annotating—see tip #42). Then give your personal reaction. Some questions you could answer:

- Did you believe what you read?
- Did you agree or disagree?
- Did you want any information that was not mentioned?
- Did it remind you of anything you read or heard about somewhere else?

This kind of journal will be especially useful if you are a student and are preparing to write or discuss the information that you read.

❧ 45 ❧

MAKE OUTLINES

When reading an article for a class assignment, take notes by making an outline of each paragraph, section, or chapter. This is a good way to remember and review important information and examples.

Here is a very simple outline format:

> I. Topic sentence
>   A. idea
>   B. idea
> II. Topic sentence
>   A. idea
>   B. idea
> III. Topic sentence
>   A. idea
>   B. idea

You can, of course, include more detail:

I. Topic sentence
   A. idea
      1. example
      2. example
   B. idea
      1. explanation
II. Topic sentence
   A. idea
      1. explanation
   B. idea
      1. quote
      2. example

Try to use vocabulary from the reading that you think is important in the outline. Highlight the vocabulary.

❧ VI ❧
READING FOR PLEASURE

❧ 46 ❧

WATCH MOVIES WITH SUBTITLES

Watch a movie in a language you don't know, which has English subtitles. The pictures in the movie will help you with comprehension.

You can also watch a movie in English that has been closed-captioned. Closed captioning provides subtitles in English for native speakers who are hard-of-hearing. Closed captioning is available on many streaming services. Then you will be practicing listening comprehension at the same time!

✢ 47 ✢

READ SONG LYRICS

Listen to a song on YouTube or another video site that has the lyrics printed in English. You can also find, copy, and print out lyrics from another site, and then read them as you listen to the song.

Read the lyrics as you listen to the song. Then sing along!

Because songs are a kind of poetry, you might find some non-standard grammar and word usage. Don't let that bother you; word play is common in every language.

Note: Be careful! Some videos might have the words written incorrectly. If you aren't sure, check a few different online sites for lyrics.

❦ 48 ❦

START AN ENGLISH READING
CLUB

Start a reading club with some friends or classmates. Choose one book to read each month, and meet weekly to talk about the book.

You can also set up a blog or shared Google doc for the reading club, if people want to write about what they think.

If you can't meet in person, then meet online, using a platform such as Zoom. That will let you have members who don't live in the same place.

To find a book for your club, check out tip #12.

❧ 49 ❧

FIND AND FOLLOW AN AUTHOR
YOU LIKE

If you like a book/article, find other books/articles by the same author.

Many contemporary authors have their own websites these days, which you can subscribe to. You'll get notified when they have a new book out, but you might also get interesting articles and even bonus scenes (content that is not published anywhere else).

You can also subscribe to the newsletters of many publishers (including Wayzgoose Press! although, to be honest, we do not send very frequent emails).

Some retail sites for books also suggest related books—if you liked X, you might also like Y. This is a good way to discover other authors that you will like too.

❧ 50 ❧

JOIN AN ONLINE BOOK CLUB

Look for an online ESL book club you can join. This way, someone else will choose the book and guide the discussion —all you need to do is read the book, and then share your opinions.

To find a free ESL book club, search for just that—"free online ESL book club."

This library has an online ESL book club in 2023; if it is no longer active when you read this book, then search for something similar:
https://www.schlowlibrary.org/events/1525

This site has very well organized ESL book clubs. However, note that is not free.
https://www.bookclubschool.com/

This site has professionally run ESL book clubs at different levels. It is not free, but you do have the advantage of a

teacher working with you (over Zoom) and classmates at your level. Courses typically last five weeks and run at different times throughout the year.
https://www.bookclubschool.com/

If you are an advanced reader or want a challenge, you could look for a reading club for native speakers.

You can search for book clubs by genre or topic (for example, "online book club" + mysteries") or even by specific title if it is current ("online book club" + *Dreamland*).

BONUS TIP!

VISUALIZE

Create a mental image of what you are reading, especially important parts of the story. Try to see the verb actions or the face of characters in your mind. This will make reading more enjoyable and help you remember scenes in the story.

Made in the USA
Las Vegas, NV
03 October 2024

96239708R00049